Daniel Boone

Janet Riehecky

RAINTREE
STECK-VAUGHN
PUBLISHERS
RSVP®

A Harcourt Company

Austin   New York
www.raintreesteckvaughn.com

Published by Raintree Steck-Vaughn Publishers, an imprint of Steck-Vaughn Company.

Project Editors: Sean Dolan, Leigh Ann Cobb, Sarah Jameson
Production Manager: Richard Johnson
Designed by Ian Winton
Picture Researcher: Rachel Tisdale

Planned and produced by Discovery Books

Library of Congress Cataloging-in-Publication Data
Available upon request

ISBN 0-7398-5672-3

Printed and bound in China
1 2 3 4 5 6 7 8 9 0 07 06 05 04 03 02

Acknowledgments
The publishers would like to thank the following for permission to reproduce their pictures:
Cover: Peter Newark's American Pictures; p. 4 Corbis; p. 5 Mary Evans Picture Library p. 6 Bridgeman Art Library/Christie's
Images; p. 7 Peter Newark's American Pictures; p. 8 Virginia Historical Society; pp. 9 & 10 Peter Newark's American
Pictures; p. 11 North Carolina Office of Archives and History; p. 12 Library of Congress; p. 13 The Anschutz
Collection/William J. O'Connor; pp. 14 & 15 Corbis; p. 16 Peter Newark's Western Americana; pp. 17 & 18 Peter Newark's
American Pictures; p. 19 Kentucky State Parks; p. 20 Discovery Picture Library; p. 21 Smithsonian American Art Museum,
Washington D.C./Art Resource, NY; p. 22 Archiving Early America; p. 23 Corbis; p. 24 Library of Congress; p. 25 Peter
Newark's American Pictures; p. 26 University of Chicago; p. 27 The Granger Collection; p. 28 Mead Art Museum, Amherst
College/Stephen Petegorsky Map on p. 29 by Stefan Chabluk.

CONTENTS

KIDNAPPED!

It was Sunday afternoon, July 14, 1776. In Boonesborough, Kentucky, this was a day to worship and to relax. Daniel Boone was taking a nap in the fort. All of a sudden, screams ripped through the air. Three teenage girls, including Boone's own daughter, Jemima, had taken a canoe out on the Kentucky River. When the current pulled them too close to the opposite shore, five Indians jumped out and threatened them with knives.

Their cries, however, had alerted the fort. Boone organized and led a rescue party. At first the Indians traveled quickly. Boone couldn't catch up, but no one on the whole frontier was better at following a trail. Gradually the rescue party got closer. By the third day, the Indians thought they were safe. When they stopped to eat, Daniel and the other men surrounded the camp, then attacked. The three girls were saved.

One of Daniel Boone's most famous adventures involved rescuing his daughter Jemima and two of her friends who had been kidnapped by Indians. He tracked them for several days, before finally catching up with them.

THE LEGEND OF DANIEL BOONE

Hundreds of stories have been told about Daniel Boone. He never wore a coonskin cap, but he was a pioneer, an expert marksman, and a skillful hunter. The kidnapping adventure really happened, but many of the stories of Daniel Boone, told in books, films, and TV programs, are exaggerated.

A FREEDOM-LOVING CHILD

Daniel Boone was born on November 2, 1734, in Exeter, Pennsylvania. He was the sixth child of Sarah and Squire Boone. His family were Quakers and had come to America from England to gain religious freedom. Squire Boone was a weaver and farmer and also owned a blacksmith shop.

This painting of a busy country fair in Pennsylvania dates from 1824. From the age of 10, Daniel was given the task of looking after his father's herd of cattle during the summer months.

THE QUAKER RELIGION

The Quakers are a Christian religious group and believe that a person does not need a priest or minister to have a relationship with God. They value simplicity, honesty, and integrity and are strongly against violence of any kind. Quakers were persecuted in Europe in the 17th century, and thousands fled to a new life in America. The Quakers were so-called because they would sometimes "quake" or tremble in their religious meetings. The man in this painting is quaking and has lost his hat.

As a child, Daniel loved to wander and explore. When he was 6 years old, his mother kept him in the house because of a smallpox epidemic. He and his sister Elizabeth did not like having to stay inside. They decided the only way to get free again was to catch the disease and get it over with.

One night they crept out of the house and went to visit a sick neighbor. They crawled into bed with the child, stayed a few minutes, and then came home. Before long, they too broke out in a rash. Fortunately, the two children recovered. It would never be easy to keep Daniel Boone in one place.

OFF TO WAR

In 1750, the Boone family left Pennsylvania and moved to North Carolina, a trek that took over a year. Daniel was 15 years old.

He helped his father farm, but he was always more interested in hunting. That fall he went into the mountains for several months on his first long hunt. For the rest of his life, Daniel would rarely miss a hunt during fall and early winter. The meat would feed the family, and the furs could be sold. He became an excellent marksman and hunter.

The Blue Ridge Mountains extend across parts of Virginia, West Virginia, North Carolina, South Carolina, and Georgia. When Boone's family lived in North Carolina, there were only a few towns scattered throughout this area.

In 1755, the British and their colonies were at war with the French and their Indian allies. Major General Edward Braddock recruited colonists for the British side in the war, and Boone

His American troops, including a young Virginian named George Washington, warned Braddock that the Indians would not march out in neat rows to fight, as armies did in Europe, but would hide behind trees and shoot. Braddock refused to listen.

volunteered to drive a wagon with army supplies. Ignoring warnings, Braddock led his men into an ambush in the forest near Fort Duquesne in Pennsylvania. Almost 900 of his men were killed. Boone escaped by cutting a horse loose from his wagon and riding it to safety.

THE FRENCH AND INDIAN WAR (1754–1763)

This was the last of four North American wars fought between the British and the French, with their Native American and colonial allies. It was part of an international power struggle between the two nations, with fighting in Europe and even as far away as India.

DANIEL BOONE, HUNTER

Boone returned from the war and in 1756 married 17-year-old Rebecca Bryan. They lived in North Carolina, where Boone farmed and hunted in order to feed his growing family. They would eventually have 10 children.

Boone traveled as far as eastern Tennessee on hunting expeditions, and tales of his skill spread among the other hunters. His name even found its way into the slang of the Tennessee mountain region, where a good hunter was called a "Boone."

> Know All Men By These Prents that Daniel Boone hath Deposited Six, vi, beaver Skins in my keep in good order and of the worth of vi shillings each skin and i Have took from them vi shillings for the keep of them and when they Be sold i will pay the balance of XXX shillings for the whole lot to any person who presents this certificate an delivers it up to Me at My keep Louisville falls of Ohio May 20 1784   John Sanders

This is a receipt given to Daniel Boone for beaver skins in 1784. Though Boone was a skilled hunter, he was not a good businessman and frequently fell into debt.

Unfortunately, Boone's skill didn't make him much money. Boone bought the items he needed for a long hunt from local merchants on credit. But sometimes Indians caught him on their hunting grounds and took all his furs, so he couldn't repay his debt. In fact, Boone spent much of his life getting into debt and trying to get out of it again.

In 1763, Boone met Richard Henderson. Henderson sued Boone several times for debt, but he also seemed to admire him. He had some ideas about starting a colony in the Kentucky territory and wanted Boone to explore the land for him.

Richard Henderson (right) was a lawyer and a judge. He sponsored several of Boone's trips to explore the frontier and also hired him to build the Wilderness Road.

THROUGH THE CUMBERLAND GAP

Between 1763 and 1769, Boone made a series of expeditions in Tennessee and Kentucky. In 1764, he met with some Cherokee Indians and discussed the sale of some of their land in Kentucky.

The Cumberland Gap was an opening, or pass, between peaks in the Appalachian Mountains. It had been used for generations by various Indian nations. For the pioneers, it provided a way through the mountains and into Kentucky.

By now Boone was anxious to leave North Carolina. Game was becoming hard to find and the taxes were too high. One day in 1768, John Findley rode up to his door. Findley had once told Boone great stories about Kentucky and knew of a trail called "The Warrior's Path" that led through the Cumberland Gap, in the Appalachian Mountains, and into Kentucky. The following year, Boone talked Richard Henderson into funding another expedition. Boone, Findley, and four other men set off on June 7, 1769.

This painting by William Ranney depicts Boone's first glimpse of Kentucky. Boone was delighted at the sight of its rich, rolling hills and wide expanse of forest.

As Boone stood in the Cumberland Gap, he was not disappointed at what he found there. He and the others spent seven months exploring and trapping. Despite being ambushed by a group of Shawnee Indians, who took all their furs and equipment, Boone loved Kentucky and was able to send two loads of furs east. He returned to North Carolina in 1771, determined one day to settle his family in Kentucky.

Towering Cliffs

"The aspect of these cliffs is so wild and horrid, that it is impossible to behold them without terror."

Daniel Boone describing the Appalachian Mountains, *The Adventures of Colonel Daniel Boon* [sic], 1784

"A Leaf Carried on a Stream"

Finally, on September 25, 1773, the Boones and five other families packed up and headed out to Kentucky. On October 9, only a day's journey from the Cumberland Gap, Indians attacked, killing four men. Boone's oldest son, James, was taken prisoner, tortured, and killed.

D. Boone

Despite the tragic event, Boone wanted to continue. He had sold his home and had nothing to go back to. But no one else was willing, so the expedition headed back east. Daniel and his family were offered a cabin in Virginia and stayed there for the next two years.

This illustration appeared in one of the first biographies of Boone. The smaller scene depicts the frontiersman fighting an Indian over the body of his dead son.

The Worst Melancholy

In a letter, Boone described his son's death as *"the worst melancholy of my life."* He wrote, *"James was a good son and I looked forward to a long and useful life for him, but it is not to be. Sometimes I feel like a leaf carried on a stream. It may whirl about and turn and twist, but it is always carried forward."*

During that time, Boone was recruited by the Virginia militia to lead a rescue party for a group of surveyors in Kentucky. He covered almost 800 miles (1,290 km) in just 61 days. The men were found and taken to safety. When Boone returned to Virginia, he was placed in charge of the defense of three forts and rewarded with the rank of captain.

On the frontier, there was a constant danger of Indian attack. Daniel Boone lost two sons and a brother to them. He was captured several times himself but always managed to get free.

A Road in the Wilderness

During all this time, Boone never gave up his dream of moving to Kentucky. When Henderson approached him in 1775 about going on another expedition, he immediately agreed.

Boone arranged for Henderson to purchase 90,000 square miles (233,000 sq km) of Kentucky from the Cherokee Indians. In return, Henderson gave Boone a land grant of 2,000 acres (800 ha). Henderson intended to form his own colony. However, to encourage families to move there, some sort of road was needed to cross the mountains.

Daniel was hired to lead a crew of 30 men in clearing the forest to create what became known as "the Wilderness Road."

Boone and his men cleared, leveled, and marked the Wilderness Road. Eventually more than 200,000 settlers would use it to travel west over the Appalachians into Kentucky.

Log cabins like this one dotted the frontier. Boone built several such cabins for his family, but on his own trips of exploration, he made do with simpler housing, such as a bedroll under the trees.

The road followed old buffalo tracks and Native American paths. When complete, it extended more than 250 miles (400 km) from Tennessee through the mountains and into Kentucky. It formed the principle route for settlers going west, and in 1926 became a section of U.S. Route 25 (Dixie Highway).

Boone's leadership skills were needed all along the way. The work was hard; Indians attacked and some men ran away. Those that stayed only did so because they trusted Boone.

Never Lost

When asked if he had ever been lost, Boone replied, *"I can't say as ever I was lost, but I was bewildered once for three days."*

BOONESBOROUGH

The road-cutters reached the banks of the Kentucky River on April 1, 1775, and quickly built a few cabins. They called their settlement Boonesborough, to honor Boone's leadership.

This famous painting by George Caleb Bingham is called Daniel Boone Escorting Settlers Through the Cumberland Gap. *It was painted in 1852, more than 30 years after Boone's death.*

Taking the Land

"Now is the time to flusterate [sic] the intentions of the Indians, and keep the country whilst we are in it. If we give way to them now, it will ever be the case."

Daniel Boone in a letter to Richard Henderson, April 1, 1775

Henderson had grand ideas for himself in the new colony. He didn't intend to let the people vote for most of their leaders or allow them to own their land outright. Instead, he and his two partners would appoint all officials. Most of the settlers did not like this idea.

In September of that year, Boone brought his family to Boonesborough. It was a difficult life. They were about 300 miles (480 km) from the nearest big settlements. There was not enough food, and there was the constant danger of Indian attacks. Many settlers gave up and returned east, but Boone was determined to stay. When Henderson returned to the east temporarily, he left Boone in charge.

LIFE IN A FORT

Frontier forts were constructed with huge logs, stacked on top of one another to form a strong structure. They were self-contained for protection from enemies and usually had sleeping quarters, a kitchen, storehouse, and a large open space for training militia. The few women at Boonesborough did all the

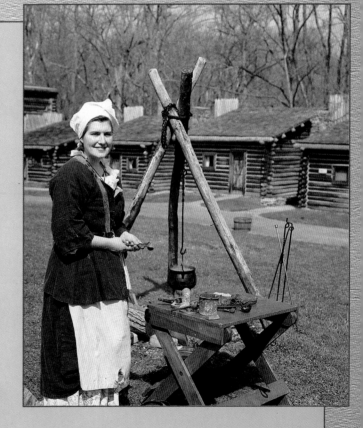

cooking and washing. Mending clothing was important because there were no stores nearby to buy new clothes or cloth. This woman is dressed in the costume of Boone's day. She stands in the middle of Boonesborough, which has been reconstructed as a working fort for people to visit.

CAPTURE!

Despite Indian attacks, food shortages, and the Revolutionary War, Boonesborough grew. In January 1778, the food shortage became a serious problem. The settlers needed salt to preserve what little meat they had. Boone took 30 men to the saltwater springs at Blue Licks. They spent several weeks there boiling the water to extract salt.

The fort in Boonesborough provided some protection from Indian attacks, though it was besieged several times. Boone reported that during one six-week period the settlers had skirmishes with Native Americans nearly every day.

This portrait by George Catlin shows Open Door, the Prophet, brother of the Shawnee Indian chief Tecumseh. When Boone was held captive by the Shawnee, he adopted their dress and body paint for a few months.

While away from the camp, Boone was taken prisoner by Shawnee Indians and learned they were planning to attack Boonesborough. He knew the fort could not survive an attack. He made a deal with the Indians and persuaded his men at the springs to surrender.

While held prisoner, Boone was adopted by Chief Blackfish and given the name Sheltowee, meaning "big turtle." He pretended to be satisfied with his life there so they would not watch him too closely. But in June 1778, he managed to escape.

RUNNING THE GAUNTLET

Prisoners taken by Indians were often required to run about 100 yards (90 m) between two rows of Indians who struck them with clubs and tomahawks. Some made it to the end. But others died. When Boone was made to "run the gauntlet," he escaped serious injury by running in a zigzag pattern. His bravery impressed the Indians.

SIEGE

Once free, Boone made his way back to Boonesborough. He covered 160 miles (257 km) on foot in less than four days to warn the settlers about the upcoming Shawnee attack. When he arrived home, he learned that Rebecca had taken the younger children back to North Carolina. She thought he was dead. Boone decided to stay and help defend the town, before going back east to find his family.

The story of the siege at Boonesborough was one of many adventures described in John Filson's biography of Daniel Boone. Filson claimed the book was in Boone's own words, but the language is clearly that of an educated man. This is the first page of the biography, which was published in 1784.

THE
ADVENTURES
OF
COLONEL DANIEL BOON,
FORMERLY A HUNTER;
Containing a NARRATIVE of the WARS of
KENTUCKY.

CURIOSITY is natural to the foul of man and interefting objects have a powerful influence on our affections. Let thefe influencing powers actuate, by the permiffion or difpofal of Providence, from felfifh or focial views, yet in time the myfterious will of Heaven is unfolded, and we behold our conduct, from whatfoever motives excited, operating to anfwer the important defigns of heaven. Thus we behold Kentucky, lately an howling wildernefs, the habitation of favages and wild beafts, become a fruitful field ; this region, fo favourably diftinguifhed by nature, now become the habitation of civilization, at a period unparalleled in hiftory, in the midft of a raging war, and under all the difadvantages of emigration to a country fo remote from the inhabited

The settlers worked on repairing the fort. In early September, the Shawnee sent a force of over 400 warriors against Boonesborough. Chief Blackfish, who had adopted Daniel, put up a truce flag, so they could talk. He promised the settlers that if they surrendered, no one would be killed.

Daniel refused to surrender, even though he had only about 60 men, 12 women, and 20 boys to defend the fort. They worked out a treaty, but during its signing a fight broke out. Once shots were exchanged, there could be no peace.

About fighting Indians, Boone said, "I am very sorry to say that I have ever killed any, for they have always been kinder to me than the whites."

For almost two weeks the Indians camped outside the fort, attacking whenever they could. They began tunneling under the fort's walls and even tried to set it on fire. Fortunately, it rained every night, so the camp did not burn. Then, on September 18, the Indians retreated. They had lost nearly 40 warriors.

ON TRIAL

During the time Boone had been a prisoner of the Shawnee, Colonel Richard Callaway had been in charge of Boonesborough. He was jealous of Boone. After the siege, Callaway brought charges against Boone, claiming he had betrayed his men to the Indians. Boone was arrested and imprisoned in a blockhouse at Logan's Station nearby. He was angered and saddened by the charges.

Daniel Boone

Boone received little formal education, but he could read and write, although he frequently misspelled words. He even spelled his last name two different ways, both with and without the "e" at the end.

Fateful Encounters

In his time on the frontier, Boone had several encounters with people whose names would be famous in American history. For example, while Boone served with General Braddock in the attack on Fort Duquesne, one of Braddock's aides was George Washington. Later, the grandparents of Abraham Lincoln were among the settlers Boone brought to Kentucky.

After his trial, which greatly upset him, Boone was free to return to life as a hunter and pioneer. This portrait of Boone, by Robert Lindneux, was painted a long time after Boone's death.

At Boone's trial, lies and exaggerations were told about him. But Boone explained his reasoning in simple, honest terms. He had done everything he could to protect Boonesborough and the outcome of the siege was proof of his loyalty. He defended himself in court so successfully that he was not only acquitted but promoted to major for "his brave actions in saving the settlements from destruction."

After the trial, Daniel headed east. He found Rebecca and his family with her uncle in North Carolina, but it took him a year to persuade his wife to return to Kentucky.

Missouri

In 1779, Boone settled his family near Boonesborough, at a place he founded called Boone's Station, near what is now Athens, Kentucky.

> In this letter from Daniel Boone to Colonel William "Cristen" (Christian), dated August 1785, Daniel talks of plots of land he has found in Kentucky. He asks for payment from the colonel, explaining he is "scarse of cash."

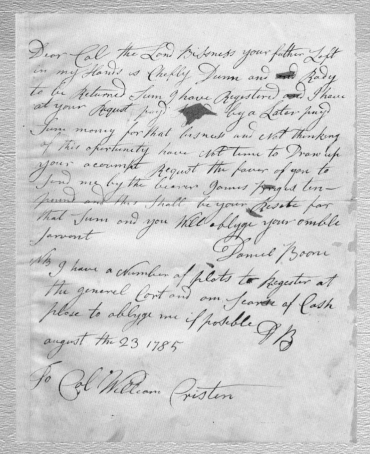

He continued to hunt and scout, as well as raise corn, tobacco, cattle, and horses. In April 1781, he was elected district representative to the Virginia State Assembly.

Peace and Safety

"Two darling sons, and a brother, have I lost by savage hands, which have also taken from me forty valuable horses, and abundance of cattle. Many dark and sleepless nights have I been a companion for owls, separated from the chearful [sic] society of men, scorched by the Summer's sun, and pinched by the Winter's cold . . . [but] I now live in peace and safety, enjoying the sweets of liberty, and the bounties of Providence."

Daniel Boone to John Filson, 1783

He tried various business ventures but was not very successful. Land in Kentucky had been given to many people without proper authorization or accurate surveys, and many of Boone's land claims were disputed. In 1798, he was forced to sell all his land in Kentucky to pay debts and back taxes.

This engraving by James Otto Lewis was published just after Boone's death. It was the first published picture that showed the type of clothing worn by American frontiersmen. Lewis copied this portrait from a painting by Chester Harding.

In 1799, Boone decided to move to Missouri, and at the age of 64, in exchange for 850 acres of land, he led yet another group of settlers to a new frontier. He gained great respect in Missouri, where he lived until his death on September 26, 1820.

THE LEGACY OF DANIEL BOONE

There have been hundreds of stories told about Daniel Boone. Many have been exaggerated or completely made up, but even just the bare facts of his life reveal that he was a remarkable man. In an age of greed, he tried to do what was right even if it hurt him. He told his grandchildren, "Never miss a chance to do good."

This 1826 painting by Thomas Cole shows Boone alone in the wilderness. Boone became famous worldwide when the great English poet Lord Byron wrote about him in his epic poem Don Juan.

Though he had reason to hate Indians, he never did. He mixed freely with them and learned from them. He claimed that in his life he killed only three Indians, in self-defense. His skill and leadership made possible the Wilderness Road that opened up the West for settlement.

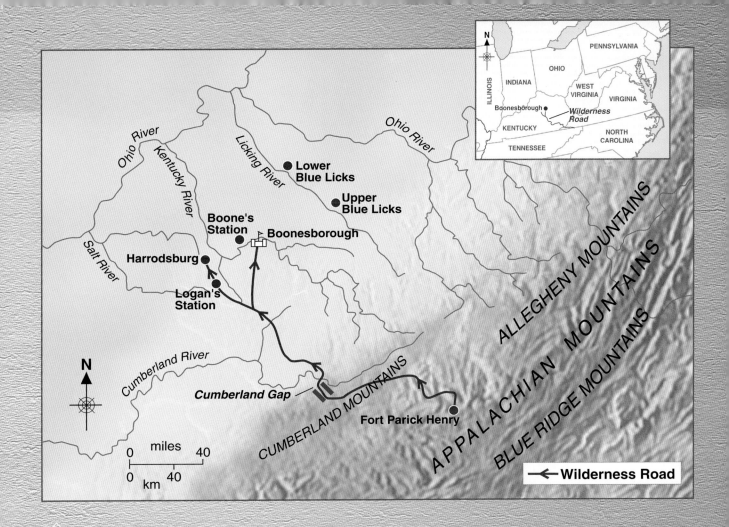

The main map shows the Wilderness Road snaking across the Appalachian Mountains and through the Cumberland Gap into Kentucky. The small map shows the present-day state boundaries, which did not exist in 1775 when the Wilderness Road was built.

He never boasted about his achievements, but said, "Many heroic actions and chivalrous adventures are related of me which exist only in the regions of fantasy. With me the world has taken great liberties, and yet I have been but a common man. It is true that I have suffered many hardships and miraculously escaped many perils, but others of my companions did the same." He remained a plain, simple man until the end of his life.

TIMELINE

November 2, 1734—Daniel Boone was born in Exeter, Pennsylvania.

1750—The Boone family leaves Pennsylvania and moves to Virginia.

1751 or 1752—The Boones settle in the Yadkin Valley, North Carolina.

1755—Daniel serves under General Braddock during the French and Indian War.

August 14, 1756—Daniel marries Rebecca Bryan.

1759—Daniel moves his family to Virginia.

1763-1769—Daniel makes a series of expeditions exploring Tennessee and Kentucky.

1766— Daniel moves his family back to North Carolina.

September 25, 1773—The Boones and five other families pack up and head for Kentucky.

October 9, 1773—Indians attack the party, killing Daniel's son James. The families return east.

March 10, 1775—Daniel begins work leading a road crew building the Wilderness Road.

1775—Daniel founds Boonesborough and moves his family there.

July 14, 1776—Daniel's daughter Jemima is kidnapped.

February 3, 1778—Daniel taken prisoner by the Shawnee.

June 16, 1778—Daniel escapes and returns to Boonesborough.

September 7, 1778—The Shawnee begin their siege of Boonesborough.

September 18, 1778—The Shawnee withdraw.

October 1778—Daniel is put on trial, but found not guilty.

November 1781—Daniel is elected as the county's representative in the Virginia Assembly.

1784—Publication of *The Adventures of Colonel Daniel Boon: Formerly a Hunter.*

1798—Daniel sells most of his land in Kentucky to pay debts and taxes.

1799—Daniel moves his family to Missouri.

1800—Daniel is appointed syndic, or judge and jury, for his district.

1813—Rebecca Boone dies.

September 26, 1820—Daniel Boone dies in Missouri.

GLOSSARY

Alert (uh-LURT) To warn or make aware.

Blockhouse (BLOK-HOUSS) A structure of heavy timbers used for military defense.

Colony (KOL-uh-nee) A group of people living in new territory that belongs to a parent country.

Confine (kuhn-FINE) To keep within a certain place.

Epidemic (ep-uh-DEM-ik) A spreading of disease to a lot of people.

Expedition (ek-spuh-DISH-uhn) A journey of exploration.

Frontier (fruhn-TIHR) A place beyond the edge of settled communities.

Integrity (in-TEG-ruh-tee) Having honesty and trustworthiness.

Marksman (MARKS-muhn) Someone skilled at shooting.

Militia (muh-LISH-uh) Men trained to be soldiers.

Persecute (PUR-suh-kyoot) To harm people, usually because of their religious beliefs.

Pioneer (pye-uh-NEER) A person who first settles a territory.

Revolutionary War (rev-uh-LOO-shuhn-airy WOR) The war fought by American colonies for independence from Britain.

Siege (SEEJ) The act of an enemy surrounding a city or fort to cut off their supplies and force them to surrender.

Tomahawk (TOM-uh-hawk) A light axe used as a handweapon by Native Americans.

Volunteer (vol-uhn-TIHR) A person who offers to work without being paid.

FURTHER READING AND INFORMATION

Books to Read

Greene, Carol. *Daniel Boone: Man of the Forests*. Danbury, CT: Children's Press, 1990.

Raphael, Elaine, and Don Bolognese. *Daniel Boone: Frontier Hero*. New York: Scholastic, 1996.

Sanford, William R., and Carl R. Green. *Daniel Boone: Wilderness Pioneer*. Springfield, NJ: Enslow Publishers, 1997.

Videos

Daniel Boone: Ken Tuck E, pilot for the 1964 television series. 20th Century Fox, 2000.

Daniel Boone—A Great American Legend (1980). Simitar Video, 1999.

DVD

Daniel Boone: Trail Blazer. Brentwood Communications, 2001.

INDEX

25

AUG 1 6 2003